I Knew I'u Done Nothing Wrong

Life as a Gay Christian in Cumbria, 1940s to 2020s

Stan Blacklock

First published 2024
by Stan Blacklock

Text and photographs copyright
© Stan Blacklock 2024

Paperback Edition
ISBN: 978-1-913898-87-8

Cover and Book interior
www.pixeltweakspublications.com

To Mildmay Mission Hospital, London, for their unwavering support in the late 80s when Fred was diagnosed with AIDS. In a time when fear and stigma surrounded this little-understood and devastating disease, your compassion and care provided immense comfort and strength. I am forever grateful.

Acknowledgements

I would like to thank all the NHS staff who have cared for me so well all my life, starting when I had meningitis and rheumatic fever as a child and continuing over the years with major heart surgery, a quadruple bypass in 2022, and now with ongoing age-related issues. These days, I get around with the aid of a walker and my heart is still being monitored by  the Cardiology Team at Penrith Hospital. I really appreciate their kindness and continued support. Having been a nurse myself, I know how hard they work and some of them regularly go above and beyond their job descriptions to help their patients.

I also want to mention the NHS AIDS Support Team who helped me during Fred's illness and when he died. The district nurses, Beryl Marr and her team looked after him in our home, enabling us to stay together till the very end. I'm still in touch with many of them.

My grateful thanks to Sal Cawley, North Cumbria NHS Sexual Health and HIV Commissioning Manager; Sister Bernie Devine, Lead Chaplain, Mildmay Mission Hospital,

London; Dr Belinda Stanley; Gary Welsh, Manager of the ACE Project, Preston; Rev Canon David Sargent and team who host my coffee mornings at St Andrew's Church, Penrith; Sharon Smith, who inspired me to write about my life; Jane Fraser, from Cumbria Sexual Health Services; and Annie Wilson, freelance creative tutor. Annie introduced me to free-lance editor Kelly Davis, who helped me write this book.

Finally, I am fortunate to have a loving, caring family, many of whom I have mentioned in this book. My thanks to all of them.

VERY bEST wishes
FROM STAM
STAM BLACKLOCK
C Bllll
9/ September 24

CHAPTER 1

'Little Golden Head'

Early years on the farm, 1940s and 1950s

My earliest memory was moving to the farm when I was only two and a half, in February 1940. It was a big house so it made a big impression. Before that, we had lived in a cottage. My parents rented the farm at the foot of Carrock Fell in a remote hamlet near Hesket Newmarket. Around 1943 I started big school, leaving in the morning about 7:45am and getting back at about 4:30pm, walking all the way in my clogs.

Loning Head Farm, Haltcliffe, where I lived with my parents, Katie and John Blacklock, till I was 18.

In 1947 I caught meningitis. I was unconscious for about two weeks and woke up in Ellerbeck Isolation Hospital, near Workington, which has since been demolished. When I woke up, I didn't know where I was. I remember Matron coming and telling me I was in hospital and I was a very sick person. They were injecting me with this new drug, called penicillin, which had only just come out. From what I've been told, that is what saved me.

Then a couple of years later, when I was 12, I fell ill with rheumatic fever and was in bed for around 12 weeks, being nursed at home by my mother. Around the same time, my baby brother John was born. My poor mother had a lot on her plate! I missed school for another 12 weeks, which I thought was great, but obviously my parents were concerned. I remember Miss Flora Barrow, a retired schoolteacher, who was our neighbour, coming to visit me and helping me catch up with my lessons. After the 12 weeks I was transferred from primary school to Wigton Secondary Modern. Having been ill, I hadn't done the Eleven Plus and I'd missed my chance of going to Nelson Thomlinson school, so I had a lot of catching up to do.

I left school at the age of 15 to help out on my dad's farm, where we had no electricity, no running water, and no indoor toilet. This meant that I had to get up at night and walk to an old 'earth' at the bottom of the garden in the dark. This was during the war years, so we couldn't even use a flashlight as we had to follow the blackout rules. The Home Guard were responsible for checking that no light was visible from any window. We had a bath once a week in a zinc tub in front of a roaring fire. By this time, my brother John was three years old. He used to go in the tractor, on my dad's knee. He loved the animals and tractors and farming generally.

Following in my dad's footsteps, I would plough the field with the horses, and do the haymaking. My mother did the weekly wash in a dolly tub, then put it through a mangle to squeeze the water out. Baking was usually done on a Thursday, when she would spend most of the day baking bread and making cakes in a coal-fired oven. I loved it on the farm. Looking back, I wouldn't have wanted any other life. I used to get up at 6 or 6:30am and help milk the cows by hand. We had a herd of around 15 dairy cows. I didn't mind the early mornings because I wanted to feed the chickens and ducks and help out in any way I could.

My much-loved parents on their wedding day, Friday 13th November 1937. Mother always commented that getting married on Friday 13th didn't bring her any luck!

We worked hard but we also had a day of rest. Sunday was always respected as the Sabbath Day and only essential work was done, like feeding the animals. Sunday afternoon tea was special. Mother would get out a clean white tablecloth and set the table with her best china. There would be a spread of cakes, bread, jam, all home-made, and maybe teacakes with honey from my father's bee hives. Sunday afternoons were spent with my sister Betty going to Sunday School at the local Methodist chapel.

Dad wasn't a churchgoer but, looking back, I realise he did a lot of Christian deeds. His favourite saying was 'Do unto others as you would be done unto yourself' and that message stayed with me all my life. He was very tall with blond hair, a good-looking man. Normally he wore the old 'bib and brace' – a loose flap held with straps made of a denim-type material. Before we had a tractor, I remember watching him walking up the field, sowing corn by hand, taking it with both hands from a huge sack on his front, skilfully scattering it left and right. Later he got a fiddle drill, in which the seed was scattered from a 'bow'.

Mum also worked on the farm, milking cows and feeding the chickens. She was average height with short brunette hair, an attractive lady with a lot of friends. She liked going to whist drives and often won prizes. She usually wore a pinny and clogs with iron corkers on the bottom, but she would dress up to go out. As soon as she came home, she whipped off her smart clothes and put her 'old rags' back on.

I had some friends the same age nearby. Richard and Patrick taught me how to play cricket. I remember we got into trouble for stealing apples and pears from our neighbour's garden. Tom Richardson was very annoyed and came and told my mum and dad. They told us off but they understood that we were only kids.

I always felt different – I always preferred male company, even as a child. My mum told me off when she found me trying on her shoes and told me they were for ladies. I remember asking her, when I was quite young, why a man couldn't marry another man.

At school, I wasn't keen on any sport but I did learn to play cricket. When I went back to school after having rheumatic fever, the doctor said I wasn't allowed to play sport because I had a weak heart. This suited me really, as I didn't want to do sport in any case. I was one of the kids the PE teacher called 'the lame, sick and lazy' because we always had an excuse for not doing games.

I was very talkative in class and Miss Huggins would often say 'Little Golden Head, turning again' when she saw me turning to speak to someone. She told me off but in a nice way. She kept in touch after I left school.

For some reason, I was always very popular with the girls. People told me I was good-looking – maybe that was why or maybe it was my friendly nature. Sometimes they pursued me, even though I wasn't interested, and words fail me at times when I think about some of the embarrassing situations I got into.

I used to go to country dancing sessions at various village halls but I was a wallflower because I didn't want to get into a relationship with any of the girls. I did feel a bit isolated and left out. People would pester me to dance and it was sometimes a bit embarrassing. I always had to have an excuse ready. Some of the girls probably thought I was just playing hard to get but the truth was that it just wasn't my scene. I was a bit shy as well, which made things even more difficult. I had always known I was different – and it became more obvious in my teenage years. I was conscious of having crushes on other boys but I was still trying to fight those urges and I would never have declared my feelings for any of them openly. It wasn't easy… I didn't want to let my parents down and I didn't want to be laughed at, teased or bullied.

In my teenage years (left) with my friend Alan Wilson,
who sadly died of leukaemia at only 26.

When I was very young, I wanted to be a joiner but unfortunately I wasn't very good at woodwork. In our woodwork lessons at school, I was always being told off for not doing a good job. When I was about 15, I started working for a joiner in Silloth but it was short-lived because I realised that joinery wasn't for me. I stayed in Silloth, which I loved, and I then got myself a temporary job as a tea boy and errand boy for

John Lane Builders, who were extending Carr's flour mill at Silloth. I had to bring the guys their coffees, sandwiches and pies from Blitterlees, between Silloth and Allonby. I went by bike and I enjoyed the ride. While I was there, I saw an advert in a shop window for help that was wanted with gardening at a big house. I did that all summer, two or three nights a week. I had always liked gardening, on the farm and at school, and I seem to have green fingers. My gardening skills came in handy a few times later on.

At the end of the summer, I came home to my dad's farm and helped out again. Then I got a job at an old-fashioned ironmonger's shop in Penrith and I was known as an 'apprentice ironmonger'. This made me feel very proud, as it was the first step to having a trade. I learnt all about hammers, nails, screws and bolts. We also stocked beekeeping equipment, kitchen fireplaces, gardening tools, all sorts of stuff. It was very interesting and I worked there for about two years, until I joined the army. The manager was Mr Tom Pelter and he and his wife kept in touch with me afterwards. They were very surprised when I was sent to Paris.

CHAPTER 2

Bonjour Paris!

National Service, 1957 to 1959

National Service was gradually phased out from 1957, and those born on or after October 1939 were not required to do it. But I was born in 1938 and, early in January 1957, at the age of 18, I got my calling-up papers. This came as a shock to my parents. After all my childhood illnesses, they'd always thought I would never pass the medical test for the army, which was done at Carlisle Castle. However, I did pass and, looking back, it was the best thing that ever happened to me. Within a week or so, I got notice from the Ministry of Defence that I was to join the RAMC (Royal Army Medical Corps) in Aldershot, Hampshire. More details followed shortly, with a rail travel warrant from Carlisle to Aldershot.

The day drew near and I remember getting a hug and a kiss from my mother and saying goodbye to Dad. Trying to hold back the tears, I took the bus to Carlisle. I was leaving home for the first time, without any choice in the matter, but I was excited as well as nervous. From Carlisle, I got on the train to London. This was another first. There were lots of other young men my age, taking the same journey to do their National Service. We were all heading for Aldershot. I soon made new friends and got chatting. All was well.

It was a seven-hour journey and the train made many stops on the way to pick up other young men who were joining the Army. When we arrived at Euston, the forecourt was crowded with military police in red caps, who had been assigned to direct us onwards. We had to get the Underground to Waterloo and, again, military police directed us to the Aldershot train. Waterloo Station was full of men in khaki uniforms, who had been previously conscripted.

When we arrived at Aldershot Station, we were met by a convoy of army trucks which took us to our final destination. On arrival at the barracks, we had to register with admin. I was given an army number, 23373494, which I would never forget, and I was told that I would be known as Private Blacklock. I had to undergo a medical examination, and we were each issued with a kit bag and military clothing and an army

On National Service – I appear third from the right, hiding behind the parasol pole.
I was a bit shy!

number. Our civilian clothing that we'd travelled in had to be sent back home. We were kept busy wrapping up parcels.

Next morning, reveille was at 5:30am and we were woken by bugles playing outside the barracks. We were also told that we must write home to say that we'd arrived safely. Time went by and I got used to morning drills every day, for three or four weeks. We learnt how to salute, march in step, and so on, and we were taught army rules and regulations. We were regularly inspected, to check that we'd had a shave and our uniforms were smart and boots shiny.

The drill sergeants weren't particularly nice to us but they had a job to do. We were always addressed by our surnames, usually shouted. The food was also quite rough and ready. I

was a bit homesick but making new friends made me feel better, and I knew we were all in the same boat.

There were one or two who found it really difficult to cope but I wasn't one of them. At this point, I hadn't come out at all. But there were about three guys in my unit who were obviously queer,

Here I am in around 1957 in our barracks, with metal beds visible in the background, at the Cambridge Military Hospital. The dog belonged to the photographer.

10

Passing Out Parade, E4 Squad, 1957.

as we called them then. They couldn't cope with the situation at all and they were dishonourably discharged.

When we started our training to work on hospital wards, I was excited to learn new skills. Over three months, I learnt how to take temperatures, give injections, take blood pressure, give first aid, learn how to make up a hospital admission bed, and so on. It was all very new to me. After a few weeks, I was transferred to the Cambridge Military Hospital in Aldershot, and I was doing practical work on the wards, supervised by Captain Liddington, the ward sister, who was an army captain serving in the Queen Alexandra's Royal Army Nursing Corps (QRANC). She was very good to work with and her other role was as a sister tutor so we got very good training. She was interested in us all.

The army doctor was Captain Padgett. He gave us medical lectures and French Professor Olivier and other French doctors and consultants also gave us training.

Eventually it was time to be tested and I passed my exams to be a trained nursing orderly. The army system was very good. There was still a barrier between officers and ORs (other ranks). We couldn't socialise with each other, but we had a good working relationship. I was a private at that stage so I was on the lowest rung of the ladder.

Another new skill I learnt as a nursing orderly was how to lay out the dead, known in the army as 'last offices'. This was normally carried out in pairs so the body could be more easily and reverently handled. It wasn't a very pleasant task.

After I passed my exams, I was called to Matron's office. She was a lieutenant colonel in the QRANC. Trembling with fear, I knocked on her office door, thinking I was in trouble. But I got a very warm welcome. I was asked to take a seat and she told me that the War Office had taken over the British Hospital in Paris and I was being posted there, and that I could take 10 days leave for a home visit before my departure. I couldn't take it all in. I needn't have worried. It seemed I had done well and I was going to start a new adventure.

While I was home on leave, I received travel documents and instructions to go to Paris. At that time the train to Paris left from Victoria Station, London, and it was known as the Golden Arrow. There was a meeting place at Victoria Station called the Golden Arrow Bar. It was an 8-hour journey, via ferry, between Dover and Calais. The train was shunted on to the ferry at Dover so we didn't have to get off. We eventually arrived at Gare du Nord in Paris and I was met there and driven to the hospital in an army vehicle.

The first thing that struck me on the way was the sight of the Sacre Coeur, standing proudly on the hill in Montmartre. Then there was the roar of the Paris traffic, with all the beeping horns, and people chatting at the pavement cafés. I remember going past the Moulin Rouge and thinking 'Wow'! For a lad from the Caldbeck Fells, this was all very exciting and overwhelming. There were billboards advertising Edith Piaf, known as 'the Little Sparrow'. She had always been one of my favourite singers and I continued to follow her until she tragically died in her sixties.

I was dropped off at the hospital, in Lavallois-Peret, a western suburb of Paris, which was only a 30-minute walk from l'Arc de Triomphe. The duty officer met me at the newly refurbished hospital at about 8pm. I was tired and hungry after a long day's travel in the August heat. When I was shown to the dining room, I was amazed by the wide choice on offer. It was a proper restaurant with a French chef.

Afterwards I was taken to what were called the barracks, but they were unlike the ones I'd been used to in Aldershot. This was certainly an upgrade! At Aldershot, there were hundreds of us sleeping on metal bunks. In Paris, there were only about 20 of us and we had proper bedrooms, sharing two or three per room. We didn't have a NAAFI (Navy, Army and Air Force Institutes canteen) so we used the local cafés. We were given a salary supplement to cover our expenses so we had money in our pockets. We learnt a bit of French at the cafés and I tasted *café crème* and *croissant* for the first time.

I made friends with a French nurse and we liked going to the cinema together to see films like *The Bridge on the River Kwai* with Alec Guinness and William Holden, and *Ten Commandments* with Charlton Heston and Yul Brynner. I was amazed by the big screen and the sound effects. Compared with the little local cinema in Penrith, it was all very grand and exciting.

After a good night's sleep and a good breakfast, I was ready to meet the hospital matron who was another lieutenant colonel. She was friendly but there was a barrier between ranks and we addressed her as Ma'am. She put me at ease, telling me the history of the hospital, the hospital rules, and explaining what my duties would be. I had noticed on arrival that the hospital was set in beautiful grounds so I suggested that perhaps I could help in the gardens. She was not amused by this suggestion!

The very grand-looking Hertford British Hospital in Paris became my new home.

She pointed out that I had not been sent to perform general duties such as gardening. I had been trained to work on the wards and it would be a shame not to use my training! I was then introduced to the ward sister, an army captain from the QRANCS.

THIS HOSPITAL
OPENED IN 1879 ON ENDOWMENT
by SIR RICHARD WALLACE
FOR BRITISH SUBJECTS IN PARIS WAS
RECONSTRUCTED DURING THE YEARS 1955-57
TO SERVE AS A MILITARY HOSPITAL FOR BRITISH
TROOPS AND THEIR FAMILIES STATIONED IN
THE PARIS AND FONTAINEBLEAU AREAS
AS WELL AS TO CONTINUE THE AIMS OF
THE ORIGINAL ENDOWMENT
The
COUNTESS ALEXANDER G.B.E. D.St.J
REOPENED THE HOSPITAL FOR
THESE PURPOSES ON
3rd MAY 1957

I soon got settled in and enjoyed my work on the hospital wards. I made new friends and started exploring Paris, a city I instantly loved. I asked the matron for permission to bring my bike over from home and was delighted to hear that my request had been granted and my bike was transported free by the Army. I loved cycling through the Bois de Boulogne and to the Cimetière Père Lachaise where I visited the graves of celebrities like Oscar Wilde, Edith Piaf and Jim Morrison. Sir Richard Wallace, founder of the hospital where I had the privilege of working, was also buried there.

Ward orderlies: Brian Clark, American nurse Mia, myself and Mike Chard.

A day out in the Bois de Boulogne with colleague Mike Churchill.

At weekends, my new buddies and I would explore the bars in Pigalle, famed for their 'ladies of the night'. Pigalle was frequented by homosexuals, transvestites, ladies of the nights, politicians and other eccentrics and American military men (GIs). The bars were full of smoke. Although I didn't smoke myself, I am still suffering the effects of passive smoking years later, with asthma and COPD. Another famous night spot was St Germain-des-Prés, known as the Latin Quarter, where we found the notorious Les Deux Magots and Café de Flore (which both still exist). I was 19, a lad from the sticks in Cumberland, a bit naïve, and I didn't have a lot of money to afford the expensive bar prices, but I was overwhelmed and enjoyed the atmosphere.

On one occasion, Mr Prince, a civilian patient from Blackpool who was on holiday in Paris with his wife, took ill with thrombosis on the Champs-Elysées. He was admitted to our Military Hospital and remained there for six weeks. When he was discharged, he invited me and a colleague to a day out sightseeing in Paris as a thank you, followed by dinner at the George V Hotel on the Champs-Elysées. It was part of my role as a nursing orderly to act as medical escort to military and civilian patients on their return to the UK so we shared a

At the Eiffel Tower in Paris, with Mr Prince.

cabin on the Golden Arrow train back to London, where he was met by his family. We kept in touch and I visited him at his home in Blackpool after demob. Sadly, he passed away at an early age.

I recall once being on night duty when I took a phone call from the Duty Medical Officer (Captain Padgett) saying he'd been called to an accident on the outskirts of Paris, which involved a military sergeant who was very badly injured and pronounced dead at the scene.

Off-duty soldiers relaxing in the garden at the British Military Hospital in Paris, 1957. From the left: Ron Adams, Brian Bartlet and me. Ron lives in Aberdeen with his wife Isobel, Brian recently passed away but I keep in touch with his widow Pat.

I was warned it was a very gory sight and asked to go down and open the mortuary to receive the body, which was down a path at the bottom of the garden. Eventually the body arrived at around 2am, and I can't really find the words to describe the sight that met my eyes. I was only 18 and this was a new and very shocking experience.

Very shortly after, the medical officer arrived at the morgue and the two of us prepared the body to military standards. The coffin had to be closed, due to the severity of his injuries. His coffin lay in the morgue, draped in a Union Jack, with his beret and belt resting on top. After finishing my shift that night, Matron checked that I was all right.

I enjoyed doing practical work on the wards and the ward sister recommended me for promotion to lance corporal, which also meant a bit more money. We had no formal French lessons because it was a British hospital but there some French staff and civilian patients so I picked up a bit here and there. I regret never learning French properly but I knew enough to get by.

It was interesting to meet patients when I did ward rounds with Matron each morning. We took it in turns to do the rounds with her and she would ask us to introduce the patient and tell her what the diagnosis was. When the patient was French, things got a bit confusing!

After the round, she would go through all the information with us in the office. It was a steep learning curve, as we were having ongoing training. I used to like welcoming new patients and visitors to the hospital. One day a gentleman appeared on the ward and asked if he could speak to the ward sister. I asked if I could tell her who was calling. He said his name was Dr Caskie so I knocked on her office door and I told her there was a Dr Caskie waiting to see her. She said, 'I don't think we have a Dr Caskie' but she told me to bring him in and introduce him and return to my duties on the ward.

She found me on the ward later and told me that Dr Caskie was actually a minister from the Church of Scotland in Paris. We had both assumed he was a medical doctor so we had a bit of a laugh. She then invited me to have tea with her and Dr Caskie in her office and be properly introduced. He explained who he was and asked me where I lived in the UK. I said 'Carlisle in Cumbria' because I knew he wouldn't know where Caldbeck was. He said, 'Really? Do you know Gretna? That was my first posting as a minister for the Church of Scotland.' He mentioned the munitions factory at Annan and we talked about the church in Paris, which had been damaged in the war, and he was helping to rebuild it.

He was a very modest man and didn't tell me himself about his extraordinary escape from the Gestapo during the war, but the ward sister knew all about it and told me later. His book *The Tartan Pimpernel* describes how he was serving as a minister of the Scots Kirk in Paris when the Germans invaded in 1940. Although he had several chances to escape, Caskie stayed in France and helped Allied soldiers and airmen escape from occupied territory. The Seamen's Mission in Marseilles became the main clearing house for stranded British service-men. Despite the dangers, Caskie continued to help them escape. Eventually he was arrested, interrogated and sentenced to death at a Nazi show trial. Fortunately a German pastor intervened and he was saved from execution. I knew none of this when I first met him.

When Dr Caskie came back to the hospital he gave the ward sister two signed copies of his book, one for her and one for me. Eventually he became chaplain to the hospital and I got to know him quite well. We had a connection because he'd lived in Gretna and knew I was from Cumberland. He wrote the book to raise funds to help rebuild the Scottish church in Paris.

At that time, I used to go to the C of E St Michael's Church in Paris, near the British Embassy. It was Dr Caskie who introduced me to the Scottish Church in the Rue Bayard near the Champs Elysées. He invited me to go with some of my colleagues. The Presbyterian services were less formal than C of E. There was a big Scottish community in Paris and I soon made friends with some of them.

One of the patients I met was the original Madame Bluebell from the famous Paris Lido Cabaret Theatre on the Champs Elysées. She was a very friendly, chatty Irishwoman. She was probably in her mid-thirties, very beautiful, with dark brown hair, famous for her dancing. She left us ten tickets for the Lido and the hospital raffled them. Sadly, I didn't win one and I couldn't afford to buy one of my own.

Another visitor to the hospital was the late Wallis Simpson, who used to visit patients, without any ceremony or escort. I used to greet her and she had a pleasant smile and often said 'Good morning, young man.' If she wanted to see a particular patient, I took her to their bedside.

Lady Edwina Mountbatten also visited the hospital. I didn't yet know about her scarlet reputation and she came to do a ward round. After the ward round, she asked Matron if she could speak to some of these 'distinguished young gentlemen'.

So Matron picked out half a dozen of us, including me, and I remember standing in a courtyard outside the hospital, very casual, and she shook hands with us. She asked us each where we came from, and how we liked being in Paris. Then she turned to Matron and asked where these 'distinguished young gentlemen' slept! Matron was lost for words and muttered something about us sleeping in a disused factory over the road. We wondered if we might get a visit during the night! But that didn't happen, as far as I know.

Another visitor to the hospital was Sir Francis Rose, in about 1958. He was openly homosexual and his partner used to visit him regularly when he was admitted to the hospital. Sir Francis was admitted because he had been the victim of a homophobic attack on the Champs Elysées. He was bruised all over and he was very shaken. He was middle-aged and he dressed very flamboyantly. He spoke with a lisp and he told us that his partner would be coming to see him and they wouldn't want to be disturbed. He was an Englishman who felt he could live comfortably as a homosexual in France but the attack he had suffered showed that he wasn't safe even there.

Seeing what he had gone through made me even more reluctant to come out, as I was worried about what might happen to me if I did. I also didn't want to let my parents down, or my friends back home. I believed then that admitting my homosexuality would make them all ashamed of me. Thankfully, the law changed in 1967 and homosexuality behind closed doors became legal.

It was now January 1959, and I was due for demob around the middle of February. That meant I only had another four or five weeks before I would be leaving this beautiful city, which

I had grown to love so much. I prepared to say goodbye to the many friends I had made and thought about what lay ahead of me, back in Cumberland. Luckily my friends from home had kept in touch so I was looking forward to seeing them again.

It was a few years before I returned to Paris and much later on, in 2003, I heard that they were putting up a plaque for Donald Caskie at the Seamen's Mission in Marseilles. I was invited by the Scots Kirk to attend the ceremony with them, so I jumped at the offer. There I was delighted to meet members of Donald's family, including his niece Evelyn and his nephew Gordon, as well as Simon Lever, British Consul-General in Marseille at the time. I was able to share stories of Donald's time as chaplain at the hospital in Paris.

It was officially confirmed that I would be leaving Paris on 15th February. The day came and, with mixed feelings and a heavy heart, I said my last goodbyes and headed for the Gare-du-Nord railway station, bound for demob procedure in Alder-shot, then onwards to Euston to get the train home. I kept remembering my life in Paris and wondered how I was going to cope with the change. But the words of the RAMC (Royal Army Medical Corps) motto embroidered on our army berets, *In Arduis Fidelis* ('Faithful in Adversity'), kept ringing in my ears, and those words still guide me along life's path.

CHAPTER 3

'I Knew I'd Done Nothing Wrong'
Coming out, 1959 to 1969

When I got back to Cumberland, I renewed old friendships with people who were keen to hear about my experiences of Paris. I took some time to find a new direction and work out what I wanted to do. Eventually I found work in the menswear retail trade and did a crash course in window dressing.

Crown Wallpapers asked me to take part in a nationwide shop window display competition and I jumped at the opportunity. In Carlisle, I did a display to promote Magicote, a new paint that only needed one coat. I borrowed a mannequin from a ladies' dress shop and put her by a wishing well with some sand and stuffed seagulls. The well was full of tins of Magicote and the model was draped in one long piece of fabric, with the slogan 'One coat covers'.

About six weeks later, when I had forgotten all about it, I got a visit from the area manager telling me I had won first prize! Wow! The prize was a long weekend in Rome for two, so I invited a friend who lived near Penrith to come with me. We had an amazing time, including free guided tours of Rome. We stayed at the Hotel Continental and our favourite place was the

Trevi Fountain, where we threw coins and made wishes. Mine was to return to Rome and explore the city further. My friend's name was Lenny Western and he has now sadly passed away.

Surprisingly, about two years after leaving the Army, I got a letter from the British Hospital in Paris telling me that the hospital was being handed back to Civilian Authority. The current Military Matron and Major Carter had given up their Military Commissions and would be running the new Civilian Authority and they wondered if I would be interested in working on the ward. This offer was very tempting but after a lot of thought I declined, as I had a plan in mind to open my own menswear boutique in Penrith.

After I left school I had a few crushes on other boys but I always seemed to choose the so-called straight ones. I came out of the army when I was 20 and worked in an agricultural merchant's – and there was an openly gay guy working there. I must have had my first sexual experience with him when I was about 26. He was a clerk at the company and he was a nice guy and he took me under his wing. He was a little older but not much. He must have told me about what went on – and about men sometimes going to public toilets.

I always felt different but I didn't know why till later on in life, probably after I left school when I was 15 or 16. Going back all those years, it was a very different world. Being gay was taboo and it was swept under the carpet. I was always told that it was wrong and it wasn't accepted so I tried to live a normal life. It did go on in the 'underworld' but I was frightened and kept away from it.

After working at the agricultural retailer's for a while, I decided to become self-employed and I contacted various agencies who found me work as a mobile window dresser. I loved my job, travelling round the country, meeting new people and making new friends. I was well paid and I was able to upgrade my little Mini to a two-seater MGBT sports car.

When I was 26, I was working as a window dresser for Crown Wallpapers, travelling all over the North of England and up to Glasgow. By this time, I was going to public toilets quite often. Unfortunately, one day I got caught in a police raid. They were quite abrupt and I remember being put in a police car with another guy who had been in the toilets. They asked me if I'd been in trouble before and I said no. But when they asked the other guy, he said he'd been arrested in Leeds the day before!

I was taken to the police station, where I was fingerprinted and questioned. I was classed as a criminal and the case went to the High Court. This must have happened in about 1965, a couple of years before it became legal in 1967. Before we'd been convicted, there was a TV report about the police raid on the toilets where they said seven or eight men had been arrested. I sat in the living room, watching the news on TV with my parents and they had no idea that I was one of the men being mentioned! After the programme some neighbours commented that the police should have had better things to do.

I knew in my heart that I'd done nothing wrong because it had all been consensual but being arrested and going to Court was very frightening. The worst part was when my parents found out, which didn't happen until I was arrested at work where I was busy window-dressing. I asked the manageress to tell my parents that I had been taken into custody. I was there for a week and the Crown Wallpapers Area Manager visited me – and asked if I wanted him to visit my parents. I agreed and was grateful for his sympathy.

When I was released, I went home to face my parents. As I stepped in, my mother gave me a hug and said I'd given her a shock, though my dad was actually more sympathetic than her. However, there was a lady in the village called Dora who was a solicitor's wife and she was also a magistrate. She visited my mother and explained that this kind of thing happened sometimes and it wasn't the end of the world.

Before they let me out on two years' probation, the case was reported in the local press and some people were pointing their fingers at me, but I also got a surprising amount of sympathy. Nevertheless, I was desperately worried and frightened about having done something that was generally considered wrong. I hated the idea of being called a queer! When I was first arrested, it was around October. But the Carlisle magistrates put off my case until the Cumberland Assizes the following January.

Before the trial, I used to go out drinking with the manager from another Crown Wallpapers shop in Carlisle. His wife sometimes joined us. On one of these evenings, I was looking a bit down and they asked me what the matter was. I think I burst into tears and told them I was feeling suicidal. I explained that I had to appear in court the next morning, though I never told them what for. They were very kind and let me stay overnight at their house and continued to be supportive after they found out what charges I was facing. People talked at all the Crown Wallpaper shops I visited for work, so everyone knew about the case, but they still gave me a very warm welcome when I returned after the news report, and I'm still in touch with some of them to this day.

While I was waiting, everything was fairly normal but then the Judge sent all ten of us to prison for a week 'as a deterrent to promiscuity' and to give him time to decide what to do with us. In the prison, I was in a cell on my own. During the day, we had to sew mail bags. The food was awful but I didn't feel in any danger. It was HMP Durham and when we arrived the gates opened and one of the wardens said 'Welcome to the Palace of Varieties'.

Luckily, I got two years' probation but a lot of the others got longer jail sentences. My short time in jail actually turned out to be anything but a deterrent to promiscuity! After I got home on probation, the local paper printed an article about me and I got loads of offers posted through my door – because there were lots of people living a lie then. Some of them were men who later got married and had families.

I was worried about how people would treat me at work but they were all sympathetic. All my friends were straight but they stood by me – and someone in the street once said I was a 'TV star'!

In the lead-up to the court case, I was depressed and had a very bad Christmas. It was the waiting and the uncertainty about what would happen that affected me most. I knew I had done nothing wrong because it was all consensual and I hadn't harmed anyone. In the dark times, I relied on my faith. I'd grown up in the Church. I left for a time, during my teenage years, but returned in my twenties and have continued to be very involved with the Church, both in Penrith and in Paris.

Once the court case was over, I was on probation for a couple of years. I had to see the probation officer once a week for the first few weeks and he was also sympathetic. Even after all that had happened, I was still living in denial, to some extent. I continued seeing all my normal, straight friends. I was too frightened to go back to the public toilets so it was a deterrent in a way. I was leading a double life. I was still getting plenty of offers, due to all the publicity. As I was still young, I didn't mind the fact that these were casual flings. One guy told me, 'I've always wanted to try it, Stan' even though he normally went out with girls.

As a postscript, I'd like to mention that I finally got an official pardon in 2021, around 60 years later! Even after all that time, it still had to go through all the legal channels and the offence has now been taken off my DBS record, as if it had never happened. This has been a great relief because it often caused me embarrassment when I applied for voluntary posts and had to mention that I had a police record.

CHAPTER 4

Minding the Shop
Esquire Menswear and cafés, 1969 to 1977

In 1969 I was still working for Greenwood's, a well-known family business who had a string of menswear shops all over the north of England. They specialised in men's bespoke tailoring and they trained me in measuring skills and then appointed me as manager at their Workington branch. I now had a wealth of experience of the trade and was looking for premises to open my own men's boutique.

I found a small empty shop in Penrith, where I was well known and I was lucky enough to get the tenancy. The next thing was to prepare the shop and find a name for it. I called it Esquire Modern Menswear. My friend Keith helped me design and prepare the shop. It was completely empty at first so we had to put in all the fittings and paint it ourselves.

It was hard work but, in October 1969, I fulfilled my ambition and opened the shop. I stocked Ben Sherman shirts which sold very quickly for around £3.10 shillings each in those days. I very quickly stocked up with other men's items, like the new, trendy Levi jeans and other high-fashion menswear. Busi-

At the Esquire Menswear Boutique, Cornmarket, Penrith, 1969.

ness boomed and I started concentrating on made-to-measure bespoke men's suits.

I employed an elderly lady, Edna May, to work part-time, who loved her job. She was 70 when I took her on and it was the first paid job she'd ever had. She had private means so she didn't need to work but her husband had passed away and working in my shop gave her another life. Having her there to serve customers gave me more time to concentrate on the made-to-measure suits, for which I had to visit people in their homes.

I also attended fashion exhibitions in London, where I would order from the latest fashions on display. There was an annual display for wholesalers (known as 'the rag trade') at Earl's Court. A lot of Jewish people and homosexual men were involved in the rag trade – and I found the atmosphere congenial and all this helped give me the confidence I needed when I came out. When I was running the shop, people knew I was gay – so some so-called straight men sometimes came in to chat me up on the quiet.

The shop lease ran out after eight years, in 1977. I could have found other premises but I decided I wanted a change of direction.

However, I did continue with the made-to-measure business. For that, all I needed was the pattern books, which were supplied by the tailors. When I had an order, I would send it to the tailors, they would order the fabric and then they would send me the suit for a customer fitting in case any adjustments were needed.

Another lady came to work for me, to cover some extra hours. She was Mrs Rylands and we got on well. She had a young family and it was useful money but she also loved the work. There was a friendly, sociable atmosphere in the shop. On a Saturday, a young man called Ian used to come in to help, as the ladies were usually off on Saturdays. He was good at working in the shop. He was definitely not gay himself but I think he knew I was, and it didn't bother him.

The shop did well. I got in at just the right time in the late sixties, when men were starting to become more fashion-conscious and new fashions were coming over from America, like jeans and leather jackets. Everyone wanted to be Marlon Brando from 'On the Waterfront'!

From 1977 to the mid-1980s, I ran a café in the bus station, called the Kona Café. We stayed open till 4am or 5am on Friday and Saturday. It was a greasy spoon café with a jukebox and we did quite well. I did most of the cooking, with some staff. It became known as a late-night hangout and young people would come in after the nightclubs closed. At night, we did a reduced menu (mainly burgers and chips), teas, coffees and cold drinks, and people were queuing out of the door. During the day I had a table licence for alcohol so I could serve the odd glass of wine, but at night I knew it would cause problems to serve alcohol, as I used to get a few drunken gay suitors. I remember one asking me for a kiss and I replied, 'Not with those greasy lips!' This was all in fun really – but some of them had wives and girlfriends and it was only getting drunk that gave them Dutch courage to come and see me.

One day in the early 1980s we had some unexpected customers. In the afternoon, after the lunchtime rush, all went quiet. I was having a break with my mother and there were two or three customers in, having a cup of tea, when we noticed a big, shiny limousine parking outside the café. I remember someone saying 'Oh, it's Shirley Bassey! And it looks as if she's coming in!'

My mother fled upstairs as she was a very shy lady who didn't like being at the forefront, though she enjoyed working behind the scenes. However, the café door opened and in came Cleo Laine. It took me a while to register who it was. (Luckily no one mentioned Shirley Bassey!) Her husband Johnny Dankworth remained in the car so I asked Cleo to bring him in. I think they were on a tour to Scotland. I remember asking her why she should visit an ordinary greasy spoon café like mine. She replied, 'We only want a cup of tea and perhaps a cake, to break our journey. This is what we like – just an ordinary café.' She commented on the piece of home-made apple pie, made by my mother, who was still hiding upstairs. Cleo said she would like to meet her – so I persuaded Mother to come down. Cleo and Johnny got on well with her – they chatted

about the café and her home baking. Their visit was the high-light of our day – perhaps our year!

The Glasgow–London buses stopped right in front of the café, so we did a good trade with the travellers. It was hard work but I enjoyed it. We had the odd rowdy customer, when they'd had a few drinks, but nothing too difficult. I was living above the café and I had a couple of spare bedrooms so I also took in bed and breakfast customers. I always had a nice, new car. I was the first person in Penrith to have a Ford Probe. It was gold so it stood out and it turned heads when I went out for a drive.

At this time in my life, I didn't have a long-term partner, only a series of surreptitious one-night stands. Even though homosexuality had been legal for a while, I was still afraid of the stigma. Looking back over my life, I can't help thinking about all the chances I missed, especially in those smoke-filled bars in Paris! Nowadays, the gay community has reclaimed the word 'queer' but in those days it was still considered an insulting word.

CHAPTER 5

Finding True Love
Fred, 1977 to 1991

In October 1977, after a busy day at the Kona Café, I wanted something to eat and decided to go for a spin down the M6 motorway to the nearest service station café. There I was greeted by a young man who served me at the counter. I could tell from his smile, and the way he looked at me, that he was gay. We couldn't chat at that point because there were other

Fred working at the service station cafe, shortly after I met him.

customers in the queue behind me, so I moved over to a table with my meal.

It wasn't long before his work colleague (a woman I knew well, who knew that I was gay) came over to ask if I would give her my phone number to pass on to Fred, and could he ring me later when he finished work? I responded, 'No problem.'

Later on that evening, after he'd finished work, I got the phone call that changed my life. We arranged to meet – and it turned out that he had three days off work so I invited him to stay with me in the flat above the café in Penrith. I remember so well, it was 31st October, Halloween Night. We spent time chatting and getting to know each other. He was 24 and I was 39. He mentioned that he preferred older men so that was OK.

By Christmas we'd got to know each other well and I introduced him to my family as a friend. He got on very well with my sister Betty and my mother. I think they knew he was more than just a friend but nothing was said openly because

Fred in the garden with our friends. Left to right: Desmond, Michael and Fred. We met Desmond and Michael on a cruise.

Fred having fun at work.

homosexuality was still very frowned upon. What mattered was that they accepted him into the family. I think my father also knew about my relationship with Fred. It was never discussed but I think he accepted it, and he and Fred got on well.

As time went on, we built a loving relationship and by Christmas he'd moved in with me. As I ran a bed and breakfast, people were always coming and going; and Fred was able to travel by bus to his workplace on the M6 motorway. He was originally from Whitehaven. His father had passed away when he was an infant, and his mother had remained in the Whitehaven area. We visited her regularly and she always made us welcome. Eventually she met my mother, and they got on very well. They must both have been aware of our relationship but it was never discussed. Fred's sister Olive spent most of her adult life in London and used to visit us regularly.

We had quite a good social life in the Penrith community and felt comfortable in the local pubs and clubs. My old friends all liked Fred – he was a sociable, popular young man, who also had a lot of his own friends, both men and women, who knew he was gay and accepted him. Like me, he was a people person.

A couple of years after Fred moved in, it was nearly time to close and the staff at the café had all finished for the day. Mother and I were cleaning up when she said, 'I can smell smoke.' The kitchen was on the first floor and it turned out that we had left a chip pan on the stove. I opened the door and saw a cloud of smoke and my first thought was of Fred, who had been working a night shift and was in bed sleeping on the second floor. I ran up another flight of stairs, shouting, 'Fred, get up! Something is on fire!' When I got into the room Fred was still asleep. I woke him up and he jumped out of bed. By this time, smoke was beginning to enter the bedroom but we got back down to the ground floor safely. The fire engine had arrived – Mother had called to a passer-by to ring them earlier. The firemen had got everything under control and there was only smoke damage to the décor and we were able to open the next day.

Not long after this, I sold the café and we moved a few doors down the road

Feeling relaxed and happy as Fred and I started our life together.

and opened the Shalom Bed and Breakfast. Fred and I ran it together, though he was still working shifts at the service station café as well. We enjoyed working together and got on well with our guests. They always left nice compliments in our guest book. Mother was still involved and it brought her out a bit. Everyone loved her cakes, which made her feel proud.

Mother at the Shalom, with Kevin, who thought very highly of her. Kevin lived in Whitehaven and rented a room from me while he worked at Oasis (now Center Parcs) near Penrith. He also modelled in my fashion shows to raise money for charity.

Fred and I enjoyed plenty of good holidays and we flew to Israel, Greece, Turkey, Gran Canaria, Paris and other European cities. We went to all the art galleries, went sightseeing and found the local gay hangouts. There was a published gay guidebook so we could go on gay walks with a guide, visiting Oscar Wilde's grave in Père Lachaise *Cemetery*, Paris, for example. We spent quite a bit on our travels, but we were both working and we shared the expenses equally. Fred was a catering supervisor and earned a reasonable wage. My business was also doing fairly well.

Enjoying the sun, on holiday in Israel.

Fred in Tel Aviv

In January 1982 something dreadful happened and Fred supported me through it. At about 4.30 one morning, there was a loud knocking at the door. Fred thought at first perhaps he'd overslept and someone had come to get him up for work. But it was our local policeman and he said he had some very bad news. I stumbled out of bed and downstairs, where he told me that my younger brother John had died and he had just taken his body to the mortuary and he needed someone to carry out the formal identification. He said that strychnine poisoning was involved. John had worked on a farm, where he had access to strychnine because it was used to poison foxes.

I knew he'd been going through a bad time because he'd been having a relationship with a local young woman and they had broken up. But he'd always seemed capable of coping with life so everyone was very shocked. He was a dearly

My brother John as a young man, always happy on a tractor.

loved son, brother and uncle and seemed to enjoy working on the farm at Caterlen Hall for Jim and Mary Dent. He loved country music and followed a local band called Silver Dollar and Bob Kendal who sang country and western songs. John had many friends and was well respected. His death at the age of 32 came as a great shock, and there were many unanswered questions. His death was investigated and the inquest took six weeks to reach an open verdict, after which his body was released for burial.

For some reason, the policeman insisted that I had to break the news to my parents, who were staying in my house at the time. I knocked on their bedroom door in the early hours and told them the awful news. It was probably the worst thing I've ever had to do. My mother was grief-stricken but not that surprised because she'd had a feeling that John wasn't happy. With a lot of help from God, I was able to support my elderly parents, particularly my mother, who was broken-hearted.

In 1985, we had another bereavement. My father died very suddenly at the age of 80. He was working as a part-time gardener near Ullswater and he'd apparently been pulling potatoes when he collapsed with a heart attack. His lady employer offered him a lift to Penrith when he finished work. He picked up his tools and when she came back she found him lying on the ground. When she realised he was dead, she called the police – and they came to my house to let me know.

My mother was with me at the time and, strangely, we had both felt a little tired and ill an hour or so earlier, which must have been when he died. We had planned to go out to Carlisle but both ended up resting in bed instead, which meant that we were at home when the policeman arrived with the sad news about my father.

Twelve years into my relationship with Fred, in around 1987, Fred got ill and had to take time off work. He felt ill all summer, kept going to the doctor, getting prescriptions and taking the medicine but it did no good. The doctors couldn't diagnose what was wrong with him. No one thought about the possibility of AIDS because we still associated AIDS with New York and London, not Cumbria. Eventually he was tested for HIV. He had no counselling before the test and had to wait 10 days for the results.

When he came in and told me, he was as white as a ghost. 'I've got some results,' he said. 'I've got it, I've got it, I've got it,' and he broke down and cried. This was a big shock to us both and we had many sleepless nights, wondering how we would cope. We lived a lie for many months. When people commented on him looking ill, we made up an excuse. We couldn't tell them he had AIDS. At that time, people mistakenly thought they could catch it just by being near someone who had it, or by touching a cup or toilet seat that had been used by someone with AIDS.

Fred's illness got worse and he started losing weight and had to spend time in hospital. His managers were suspicious, and rumours eventually went round that he was suffering from AIDS. They made life difficult for him because they were ignorant and didn't understand it. He had to leave but he took his case to the union, who were very supportive and helped him win his job back. After he got the job back, he decided to leave on principle because the management had treated him so badly. Meanwhile, his colleagues were all very supportive and he remained friends with them.

We both knew he was dying. He'd been told by the hospital doctors that he only had six weeks to live. However, I looked after him at home (helped by caring district nurses, who attended him each day) and he surprised everyone by living for 16 weeks in the end. The week before he passed away, I remember driving him to Whitehaven to see his mum. She made us a lovely tea. I knew deep down that this would be his last trip to Whitehaven. He kissed his mum goodbye and I just knew that he would never be back. He was quite ill on the drive home and just wanted to get back into bed.

Towards the end, Fred was in a wheelchair but we still managed to get out with friends and make the most of the time we had.

At that time, there was still so much fear of possible infection with AIDS that the hospital insisted we kept a body bag in his room. He once asked me what it was. I couldn't bear to tell him – but I think he knew really. There was some talk about him having to be buried in a lead coffin; some undertakers were frightened to touch the bodies of people who had died of AIDS.

I called the doctor the following morning and he came out to see us and arranged for a night nurse. Later that week the doctor put Fred on a morphine syringe. This confirmed my suspicion that our time together was nearing its end. He remained in bed, though conscious, until the last few hours. I contacted his mum, told her the situation and asked if she could come through.

She didn't drive so she asked a friend to bring her. It was very stormy on 10th November, the night before Remembrance Sunday, and they had to drive through floods and diversions to get to us. My mother, who lived in a granny flat in our house, came in and said she was going upstairs to say goodnight to Fred. She came back downstairs crying and said, 'I can't go to bed yet – Fred won't be here long.' She sat with me and the night nurse.

I kept going upstairs and saying to Fred, 'Your mum's on her way.' Eventually she arrived and I let him know straight away that she was there. I took her upstairs to see him and I think he'd been waiting for her. He opened his eyes so he knew she was there, but she went straight back downstairs because she couldn't bear it. The night nurse was downstairs talking to my mum and Fred's mum. She then came up and said, 'Stan, he won't be here long so I'm going to leave you here with him.' She left us in the bedroom together and I got down on my knees and took hold of his hand and said, 'Fred, it's time to let go now.' I thanked him for our time together, and thanked God and said a little prayer. He must have been listening because at that moment he did let go. He died about midnight.

Then I had to phone the hospital and a lady came to lay him out and they used the body bag that had been waiting in his room. The next day, we had to register his death and make the funeral arrangements. His body was taken to the undertaker's in the body bag and I asked them if they could prepare him for burial but bring him back to the house in the coffin for one last night. They did that and the coffin was in the downstairs front room until the undertakers fetched it for the funeral service at St Andrew's Church, Penrith, on 14th November, followed by a blessing service at St James's Church, Whitehaven, before he was interred at Whitehaven Cemetery.

Fred's grave at Whitehaven Cemetery with the inscription 'Love is Forever'.

The funeral was well attended and there were loads of flowers. Mum and I always used to listen to *Songs of Praise* and Fred had once asked if we could have a rousing Welsh hymn called 'Guide Me, Oh Thou Great Redeemer' at his funeral – so we followed his wishes. We sang it at Penrith and played a recording of the same hymn at Whitehaven.

After Fred's death in 1991, I struggled emotionally and took time to grieve. But gradually the pain of losing him was replaced by happy memories of our time together. I appreciated the support I received from his mother Olive and his sister, who was also called Olive.

Fred's sister Olive moved from Whitehaven to London when

Olive at the Metro Centre on her mobility scooter, 2024.

she was 20 and made her home in Tooting. Unfortunately, her husband passed away but she has remained in London and regularly comes to stay with me in Penrith. She also visits her cousin Sue in Egremont and attends to the family graves in Whitehaven Cemetery. Although Olive struggles with health issues, she has a strong positive attitude and she is an inspiration to us all – my friends call her 'the lady from London'.

I also received support from many of our friends and real-ised that something positive was coming out of Fred's death. Having had a lot of help from medics while he was ill, I wanted to give something back. So, with a lot of help from Wendy, a social worker who had become my friend, I set up a support group for those affected by HIV and their friends and family members. We recruited 15 to 20 volunteers to cover the whole of Cumbria, from Barrow to Kendal and right up into the Scot-tish Borders. People were still dying of AIDS at this time and we were given a ringfenced grant by Social Services. We were called the Cumbria Support Group for HIV and AIDS, and I was asked to be Chairman. I took on the role for eight years, playing a hands-on part, visiting clients all over Cumbria. The tasks were many and varied and quite emotional at times.

We were dealing with a lot of young men who had left Cumbria and gone down to London to live as gay men. There, they caught AIDS and then came home to villages and small towns in Cumbria, where their parents had a double shock: firstly discovering that their sons were gay; and secondly find-ing out that they had a fatal illness.

Our Support Group volunteers referred them for profes-sional help. Sadly, at this point the only medical treatment available was AZT, which delayed the symptoms a bit but did not provide a cure – so very few people survived. One young man was in the hospice in Carlisle where I used to visit him. When he came home, he was so anxious to save his parents embarrassment that he changed his surname so that people wouldn't know he was their son. Another young man I supported told me his dying wish was to return to the United States and die over there. I heard later that he died very shortly after going back there.

Being there to comfort those who were dying, and their partners and family members, meant learning a lot of new skills, though I had already gained a lot of experience from nursing Fred and the nursing I'd done at the British Military Hospital in Paris. All this played a major part in helping me through the dark days. We also received local training in caring for people with HIV and AIDS. I've always believed that God has a purpose for us all and, looking back, I can see a pattern running through my time at the Military Hospital, later on caring for Fred, and finally getting involved with the Cumbria Support Group. I've always had a caring attitude and I'm a good listener and I've always followed my old Army motto: Faithful in Adversity. It's about resilience and not losing heart, persevering even when things are difficult, and always keeping a positive outlook.

One of the first things we did when we started the Support Group was to set up a helpline, managed by volunteers from all walks of life, including a retired doctor. The helpline gave people a way of getting information confidentially, which was important because people were so frightened and ignorant about AIDS and there was still a great stigma attached to it.

Those of us volunteering for the Support Group soon found that we needed support ourselves. The doctor who volunteered for us gave his fellow volunteers the counselling we needed. There were also highly trained social workers on hand to let us offload our feelings after dealing with difficult situations and heartrending farewells to clients we had come to know well.

As time went on, new drugs changed the lives of those who were infected and they were able to live longer, in good health. I resigned from the Support Group in around 2000 but still keep in touch with some of those who were infected with HIV more than 20 years ago. Some of them are now in their fifties and in failing health but have enjoyed a longer lifespan than would have been possible before the development of anti-retroviral drugs.

Having had the experience of looking after Fred and running the Support Group, I had gained a lot of knowledge of those in need and decided to expand my horizons by getting involved in other activities in the voluntary sector. One obstacle that concerned me was that I would need to have a Criminal Records Bureau (CRB) check (now known as a Disclosure and Barring Service or DBS check).

I was conscious of the offence I'd been charged with in the 1960s, which meant that I had a criminal record. After a lot of thought and prayer, I knew the offence was consensual and had been dealt with, yet it still remained on my record. I found it embarrassing, having to explain about it, but I knew it would come to light so I always mentioned it straight away in interviews.

In the 1990s, my mother's health started to decline and by 1996 she was wheelchair-bound. I looked after her at home but she was taken into hospital and unfortunately died there. We had always been very close so this was a big blow – but I drew strength from God and my faith and the people at my local church.

After Fred died at the end of 1991, I was running the Cumbria AIDS Support Group and I wanted to mark World AIDS Day and remember Fred at the same time. I decided to hold an event, to raise money and awareness, and I decided the profits would be shared between Mildmay Hospital in East London (one of the first hospitals to treat those with AIDs) and the Cumbria Support Group.

A lot of local people helped me, including a young man called Gavin from Whitehaven who became a good friend and continued helping with my events every year. He and his wife Trish still visit me regularly, and their son Gavin Junior is now in his late twenties.

Trish, Gavin and Gavin Junior in my back garden.

I first ran the event in 1992 and I have held it most years since then, sometimes in Kendal, sometimes in Barrow, Whitehaven, Penrith and Carlisle. It's normally held at a church but I have sometimes joined forces with the Soroptomists. Each year we raise a few hundred pounds and we know it's much appreciated. One year we got some funding to pay for a parade by the Barrow Barracudas, with their drums and stilt walkers, which attracted a big crowd. Another year, I joined forces with the House of Fraser to do a menswear fashion show at a hotel in Carlisle. I recruited some Penrith lads to be models and they loved it! More recently, we've had service users giving talks about their experiences. Our aim is to raise funds and awareness, as there is still some stigma surrounding AIDS even today.

Simon, one of the service users, has written the following testimonial and he has kindly given me permission to share it in this book:

> In 1996, I was working and living in Manchester, managing a city centre bar and bistro/nightclub, and that summer I came down with what I thought was flu – a very severe flu with hot and cold sweats, and a very sore dry throat. It was very hot that summer and I was eating lots of ice cream to soothe my sore throat, and I decided to go to the doctor.
>
> My doctor took bloods for an AIDS test and I had to wait a nervous week before he phoned and asked if I would go and see him. When I got to the surgery, I sat down and he told me I had tested positive for HIV. He said he wanted to start me on antiviral medication straight away, which at that time was horrible – AZT, Septrin and another drug which I can't remember.
>
> I resigned from my job and moved back to Broughton in Furness in Cumbria, where the health service put me in contact with the Cumbria HIV and AIDS Support Group run by Stan Blacklock and consisting of volunteers manning phones and providing 24-hour emotional, financial and

practical support to people affected by HIV and their families.

It was an excellent service that the NHS couldn't provide itself and it helped me immensely. It was difficult enough having to come to terms with being HIV-positive – and being told by my father to crawl back into the gutter I came from – as well as being homeless.

I was put in a homeless hostel in Kendal for two months and then I was offered a flat by South Lakeland District Council.

I had no money or savings but the Cumbria HIV and AIDS Support Group applied on my behalf to the Elton John Trust, the Lighthouse, the George House Trust in Manchester and the Terrance Higgins Trust for grants to enable me to purchase white goods, a bed and carpets.

They were great when I needed help and support.

When we first started in 1992, people were still dying of AIDS. Now, thankfully, it's very different because of medical advances. People's needs have changed. They are living much longer and leading more normal lives. Of course, I wish these advances had come in time for Fred.

CHAPTER 6

'How Great Thou Art'

My Christian faith

My faith has always been at the forefront of my life. I believe it is the rock on which I stand, in good times and bad. It helps me to achieve and accomplish my goals and has been a constant source of strength at difficult times, such as when I was accused of the offence in the public toilets and also when I lost Fred and my parents and my brother John. I feel that God listens to us all but we don't always hear Him. He's always there – and I find that very comforting. He's there in good times, as well as bad, and I thank Him for the joy I've experienced, particularly the time I had with Fred. Nowadays I enjoy going for a walk and seeing God's work all around me, in the flowers, the trees, the birds and all the beauty of nature.

As a child growing up, I always went to Sunday School, which was run by the Oldman family, who were farmers and Methodist preachers. I always enjoyed singing and loved to hear the words of lovely hymns like 'Rock of Ages Cleft for Me' and 'Let Me Hide Myself in Thee'. 'Jesus is Mine' was another favourite, and 'How Great Thou Art', particularly the words from the last verse which for me are very powerful and reassuring:

When Christ shall come, with shout of acclamation,
And take me home, what joy shall fill my heart.
Then I shall bow, in humble adoration,
And then proclaim: 'My God, how great Thou art!'

On special occasions, like Christmas and Easter, I would go to our local C of E church, and at the age of 12 I was confirmed at Caldbeck Anglican church. The local rector organised a three-month course for a dozen of us, all around the same age. We attended for religious instruction, which led up to a confirmation service.

After being confirmed, we were privileged to take part in Holy Communion and celebrate by eating the wafer (representing the body of Christ) and drinking the wine (which symbolised His blood). At my first Communion, I was very nervous – and the wine was my first taste of alcohol. I only took a sip and I didn't like it much! The rector tried to make us feel comfortable but I still felt self-conscious in my new suit. It was the first time I'd worn long trousers and the church was quite full, with a big congregation, full of proud parents and grandparents as well as local dignitaries.

During my National Service I regularly attended St Michael's Church in Paris in the Rue d'Aguesseau, which was an English-speaking church. In 1958, the new Scots Kirk was completed and it was Reverend Dr Donald Caskie, our hospital chaplain, who introduced me to the new Kirk, in the Rue Bayard, at the bottom of the Champs-Elysées.

I donated a list of incumbents, including Rev Dr Donald Caskie, which is displayed at the Scots Kirk. I had a lot of help from a church colleague, Elizabeth Sevo, who played a big part in researching all the dates and details of the ministers.

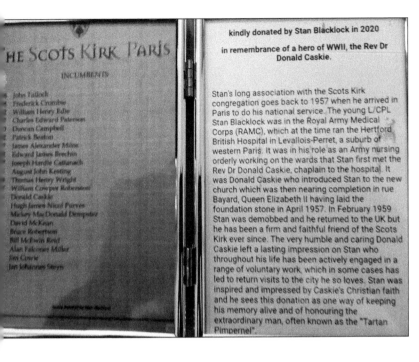

The text on the right reads:

Kindly donated by Stan Blacklock in 2020
In remembrance of a hero of WWII,
the Rev Dr Donald Caskie.

Stan's long association with the Scots Kirk congregation goes back to 1957 when he arrived in Paris to do his National Service. The young L/CPL Stan Blacklock was in the Royal Army Medical Corps (RAMC), which at the time ran the Hertford British Hospital in Levallois-Perret, a suburb of western Paris. It was in his role as an Army nursing orderly working on the wards that Stan first met the Rev Dr Donald Caskie, chaplain to the hospital. It was Donald Caskie who introduced Stan to the new church which was then nearing completion in rue Bayard,

Queen Elizabeth II having laid the foundation stone in April 1957. In February 1959 Stan was demobbed and he returned to the UK but he has been a firm and faithful friend of the Scots Kirk ever since. The very humble and caring Donald Caskie left a lasting impression on Stan who throughout his life has been actively engaged in a range of voluntary work, which in some cases has led to return visits to the city he so loves. Stan was inspired and impressed by Caskie's Christian faith and he sees this donation as one way of keeping his memory alive and of honouring the extraordinary man, often known as the 'Tartan Pimpernel'.

Rev Dr Donald Caskie the 'Tartan Pimpernel'.

After I left the Army, I left the Church for a while but Fred's illness brought me back to the Church. I still couldn't tell other parishioners about Fred's diagnosis because there was such a taboo about AIDS and people were still frightened and misinformed. But I did get good support from Mildmay Hospital when I went down to London.

When Fred was ill, I used to pray with him, especially when we knew he had little time left. He wasn't a churchgoer himself but he believed in God and Jesus. He lay there and listened while I prayed. He particularly liked the Psalms – he appreciated their poetry.

I am currently a member of St Andrew's Church, Penrith. I regularly attend Sunday morning worship and I appreciate the warm welcome I get from Reverend David Sargent and his team. I carry out certain church duties, including bereavement support. I occasionally pop into the Gospel Hall on Queen Street on a Sunday afternoon, where Keith and Marlene are always very friendly and give us all a cup of tea after the service.

I also work as a volunteer on the Chaplaincy Team at Mildmay Hospital. Our lead chaplain is Sister Bernie Devine, a Roman Catholic nun who has become a good friend as well as a colleague. She gives me my duties for the day. Just before lunch we have morning prayers in the hospital chapel, where the patients who are able also attend. I sometimes

Bernie Devine, lead chaplain.

do a reading or give a talk about my life in Paris, my prison work and other topics. Sister Bernie leads us in prayer. I always feel spiritually refreshed and inspired by Sister Bernie's words. After lunch we have board games sessions with the patients who want to take part, and normally a bingo session with small prizes, such as toiletries, for the winners. It's good fun and gets the patients motivated.

Although I'm not a chaplain, my duties include visiting patients on the ward, some of whom are very ill and nearing the end of their lives. I sit by their beds reading their favourite passages from the Bible or Psalms, holding their hands, just being there to comfort them and their families. This work can sometimes be hard and emotionally overwhelming but we have a support worker who gives us counselling and allows us to offload when it all gets too much. We also get training before we start, to help us cope with our own feelings, as well as those of the patients and their family members. Reflecting on my National Service, and my experience of working on the hospital wards, I believe that God was preparing me for what lay ahead. In 2017 I was asked to write a letter about my voluntary work at Mildmay and I said: 'My relationship with the individuals that I see is an important part of the reason why I visit. Being valued and being part of a caring team gives me the satisfaction of serving a useful purpose.'

Sister Bernie has kindly sent me the following comment:

Sixteen years ago, when I was a new 'girl' at Mildmay Mission Hospital, Stan and I bumped into each other at the annual Carol Service. On that occasion Stan expressed a wish to become even more involved as a volunteer in the chaplaincy department. Previously he had been a fund-

Winning Cumbria in Bloom for my flower display at Shalom.

raiser for a few years. I then took him under my wing or was it vice versa?

I wanted to ensure that, after travelling from Cumbria, his time with us would be productive and he would feel welcomed and, above all, cherished. I need not have been concerned. Being an exceptionally empathic listener, he communicated with patients, staff and visitors alike and of course, as a strong Christian, contributed so much to our lunchtime chapel services. We love his presence with us and among us and pray that, in spite of his senior years, we may continue to see his smiling face and enjoy his warmth, humour and generous volunteering here at Mildmay Mission Hospital.

Interestingly, I've always felt closer to God when working in the garden. It is good therapy, watching plants grow and bloom. It was fascinating growing my own plants from seed but these days I find it easier to buy fully grown plants. I love window boxes and have won several Cumbria in Bloom awards over the years.

Growing plants also reminds me of my childhood on the farm.

I am honoured to judge flowers and vegetables at four or five local agricultural shows each year. These include Penrith Show, Skelton Show, Dufton Show, and Hesket Newmarket Show.

CHAPTER 7

Making a Difference

Prison volunteering, from the early 2000s

I eventually plucked up the courage to apply to an agency for volunteering as a mentor working in prisons. I was given a week's training, which I enjoyed. It all seemed to be common sense, and my previous experience of working in the hospital and with the Support Group, and looking after Fred, meant I was already halfway there.

There were quite a lot of rules and regulations about safeguarding, boundaries and confidentiality. There was always a theoretical risk of being attacked by a prisoner but I never had any such experience. I got on well with all of them but we still had to have boundaries. For instance, they only knew my first name and only had a vague idea of where I lived.

The first prison I visited was Lancaster Farms, which was a young offenders' prison then. They had young men, aged 18 to 30, who were mainly there because they had committed drugs-related offences and petty crimes.

About six weeks before their release, I started visiting them once a week at the prison, to get to know them and talk to them about life outside, what ambitions they had (if any), and what kind of practical support they might need. Some were discharged to a supported-living hostel and others had to find their own rented accommodation. Most of them were released on licence, which meant they had to report to a probation officer regularly, and I accompanied them to these meetings and to the Job Centre and Housing Services. If they got into trouble again, they were recalled to prison, and I would attend court hearings with them. I also discussed their progress with the probation officer as far as I could without breaching confidentiality.

After they were released, I visited them regularly and provided a caring, non-judgemental, listening ear. As a volunteer rather than a professional, I was a 'friend with boundaries' and they felt able to confide in me. It was a big responsibility but very rewarding, especially when I saw these young men turning their lives around. I never tried to turn them into Christians but some of them asked me to take them to a local church, just to sit there and say a prayer, and some of them later joined a church.

A good relationship with a mentor can greatly reduce the chances of a young person reoffending, and much of this work is done through effective mentoring programmes. Each mentor is matched with a young offender to provide one-to-one support and encourage them to reach their full potential. A mentor is a guide who can help the mentee to find the right direction and believe in themselves. It should be a positive relationship built on trust, mutual respect and empathy. The offender not only gets constant practical help from someone who understands their situation but also benefits from increased confidence and self-esteem.

At this time, my working life was changing because people were no longer wearing suits so my made-to-measure business was no longer needed. I therefore applied to an agency to do merchandising and window dressing and I was employed to do window displays for 'Our Price' record shops. I travelled from Preston up to Glasgow, promoting all the latest chart releases, making many friends at the different shops. I loved the music, especially the old sixties stuff, like the Beatles, the Shadows, and the Animals, as well as American Motown records and metal bands like Black Sabbath. We also promoted videos – for independent shops and supermarkets as well as Our Price.

Eventually I got a freelance contract with Gillette Razors. Gavin, a friend from Whitehaven, helped me and we had a great time doing Gillette displays in shops all over Scotland as well as Northern England. There were no sat navs then. We had to rely on our road atlas and we sometimes struggled. On one occasion, we were looking for an Asda shop somewhere in Scotland and we kept going round in circles. Eventually we thought we'd found it, went in and I told the manager we'd come to do the Gillette display. She said, 'But you've only just left!' No wonder Gavin thought all the buildings looked familiar! I'm still in touch with Gavin and his family – they are very special friends.

In between work and volunteering, I had a good social life. I was volunteering for eight different charities at one point: SOVA (Support Others Through Voluntary Action) as a prison vistor, SSAFA (Soldiers, Sailors, Airforce and Families Association) as a caseworker dealing with active and veteran service personnel who needed to apply for financial or practical assistance, Mildmay Hospital in East London as a fundraiser, Elizabeth Finn Care (formerly Distressed Gentlefolks) as a visitor identifying individual needs and preparing paperwork for applications, Eden Community Alarms as someone who checked alarms and a visitor checking on users' welfare, the Church of St Andrews as a bereavement support volunteer, British Legion as a caseworker, and Turn 2 Us where I identified financial needs mainly for elderly, isolated people. Even though I was no longer Chair of the Support Group for HIV and AIDS, I was still connected to it and still saw the members.

Looking back, I wonder how I did it all! I suppose I was younger then and luckily my working hours were flexible and I got a lot of satisfaction from volunteering.

In 2007, my sister Betty passed away very suddenly, with a brain haemorrhage at the age of 67. She left her second husband behind, as well as three daughters and a son. I'd always loved her and she had thought the world of Fred and gave me a lot of support when he died.

My sister Betty, in her fifties.

We hadn't always seen eye to eye but that often happens in families and 'it takes two to tango'. I was particularly close to two of her daughters, Trish and Gillian, and they still help me with all sorts of practical things. They are both very caring – and always there when I need them. Their eldest sister Christine also lives in Penrith and she's busy running a Benetton shop but she also keeps in touch and I see her from time to time.

In July 2011, I was invited to a reception at the House of Lords by Baroness Linklater who was President of SOVA

In 1985, with my niece Trish, her baby son Jason, my mother and my great-niece, Christine's daughter.

(Support Others Through Voluntary Action). I was invited three or four times at yearly intervals to speak about my work as a volunteer and they provided a delicious buffet as a thank you. Other SOVA volunteers from different parts of the country also attended but I was the only one from Cumbria. The peers were very interested in our activities and asked a lot of questions about what motivated us to do our voluntary work and what kinds of people we were helping.

In around 2012, SOVA ran out of funding and had to restrict their activities to the south of England. So I took some time off and went to Paris for a few months in the summer. I did some voluntary work for SSAFA while I was there, as well as the Missionaires de la Charité, founded by Mother Teresa to help the homeless in Paris and supported by the Scots Kirk in Paris. That was quite a challenge. The hostel was near the Eiffel Tower. It was run by Catholic Brothers and the tasks there could include going out in the early mornings with a coffee wagon to wake up the homeless with a hot drink. Sometimes they would tell us to 'F__ off'! I did my hostel work every other week. I would help with laundering the bedding and preparing meals in the kitchen. I had some savings that I could live on and I'd rented out my house in Penrith, which gave me some income.

Being in Paris as an out gay man was very different from my earlier experience in the 1950s and 1960s. I used to go out drinking at clubs, socialising at parties and cafés. I had a few short-lived relationships but nothing like my previous partnership with Fred. We went to some shady places, in Montmartre. There were burlesque bars where we liked to watch drag artistes.

I came back to the UK in August 2012, looked on the Internet for voluntary work in prisons and found an organisation called Caritas Care, which was funded by the National Lottery. I had to be DBS checked and trained, and I got through all that without any problems, and joined them as a mentor in 2013. The mentoring system was exactly the same as I had previously known, and I went back to Lancaster Farms Young Offenders Centre. The service users were offered training courses in practical skills, like computer skills and catering, to prepare them for employment.

After release, some of them had problems with mental health issues, and alcohol and drug addiction, and we referred them to appropriate support services. Even though we had to take care to keep boundaries in place, we inevitably grew close in some cases – and I am still friends with some of the men who were once my mentees. Many of them had had difficult childhood experiences and saw me as a father (or grandfather!) figure. I was someone they could trust and confide in.

One of them, Michael Weir, has very kindly written a testimonial about the time we spent together and he has given me permission to use his name and words, which appear below:

I first met Stan when serving a three-and-a-half-year prison sentence in HMP Lancaster Farms, on a visit.

Stan was volunteering on behalf of the Assisted Community Engagement (ACE) project. At first I did not know what to make of him, as I had not been receiving visits from anyone and rarely got to leave my cell. I was very untrusting and didn't know why a stranger would take the time to visit the prison I was in.

For one he was much older than me, and two he had not lived the life I had lived. All I could think of was how I could get back to the wing so I could take drugs.

Over the following weeks, I remember asking Stan why he was there, and his reply was 'Because I want to help, if I can.' I remember thinking to myself 'You have your work cut out, because I am beyond help, and nothing has ever worked for me before.'

I cannot remember much more about the initial visits, but what did surprise me was that week after week I was called from my cell to see him. This caught me off guard, as no one had ever kept their word to me before. For the remainder of my sentence Stan turned up weekly. He was never intrusive, nor did he force any help upon me; we just talked about normal everyday things.

In fact for the first few visits I did not engage at all and used to sit much of the time in silence. However, those visits turned into an escape from my prison cell, an hour a week, which was a godsend when I was locked up 23 hours a day. I started to trust him more, merely on the basis that he was consistent and turned up when he said he would. This made me open up to him. As I got to know him and he got to know me, he was genuinely interested in me and my life.

I never felt judged or 'less than'. Stan told me he believed in me, when I didn't believe in myself.

Upon release I was still battling with my addiction, I was unmanageable, and I could not function without taking drugs. Nevertheless, I continued to receive support from Stan, he still turned up every single week.

He would come and find me on the streets of Preston, when I was homeless, to check if I was OK, just to have a chat and give me a hot drink. He never once gave up on me.

Together we would go on days out, across the county, visiting museums, libraries and visitor attractions. For once, someone was treating me like a human being and did not see me as a homeless drug addict.

Finally, on 20ᵗʰ December 2019, I became clean of all drugs and free from committing crime, and Stan played a massive part in that. Stan taught me some vital values throughout the time we spent together, which I take with me throughout my life. Here are a few examples of things he taught me: To be consistent – and never give up; Be reliable – if I say I'll do something I'll do it; Trustworthiness – trust goes a long way when building relationships with people; Resilience – never give up no matter what. In the time I have been clean, I have got my life back, I have my immediate family back in my life with whom I have good relationships, something I have previously struggled with, due to my addiction issues; my brother has in fact found recovery himself.

I am in full-time employment; I have travelled the world, visiting various countries; I have even taught English in a school in Africa to children from a local village, who suffer from poverty and deprivation.

I have a beautiful relationship with my long-term partner, which is a stark difference from previous relationships as my addiction issues would always get in the way and the relationships would become codependent and toxic. I have two great step-kids. One wants to follow my footsteps after coming to work with me on their work experience, and the other confided to me that he really appreciates the support and help I have given him.

I have also recently purchased a house with my partner, which we are renovating to make it into a home for our family, which absolutely blows me away, as I was homeless only a few years ago.

I will forever be grateful to Stan for the time he has invested in me and will value his friendship for ever.

I was very moved when Michael gave me this statement and I'm so glad to see how he has turned his life around. I feel lucky to have met him and would also like to acknowledge all the support I got with my volunteering from the team at Caritas Care who paid all my expenses and always lent a sympathetic ear if any problems came up.

Michael and Tamasin in Africa, 2022.

In about 2014, I started volunteering with the Assisted Community Engagement (ACE) Team. We are a small project team supporting ex-offenders who have been released from prison. Our aim is to reduce re-offending. Headed by our manager, Gary Welsh, we come under the umbrella of Recycling Lives, a leading national charity. We are on a mission to encourage and empower people to achieve positive change and improve their quality of life.

Every Tuesday, the Members After Prison (MAP) meet and this group is attended by those who have recently been released from prison. They have various needs, including practical matters such as help with benefits, finding somewhere to live and work, and managing money and their budgets. For those with mental health issues, we can refer them on to the appropriate services. The session lasts for a couple of hours and I usually attend every other week. Every alternate week, I hold a one-to-one meeting with an individual service user.

Due to my mobility issues, I am met at Preston Station by John or Amy who transport me to and fro. I feel valued and proud to be a volunteer member of such a caring team.

One of the young men I've supported through the ACE Project is Nathan Hennedy. He has sent me this testimonial to be included in this book.

I first met Stan in February 2017 when I was 21. He was a volunteer for the ACE Project.

My learning disabilities have always made me a difficult person. Add that to an enthusiasm for drink and drugs and you get a very challenging young man.

I was in a tenancy but out of my depth and unable to manage. I was using drugs and making bad choices, mixing with the wrong people and generally doing stupid things. I'd disconnected from my family.

One of the few constants was Stan. Unlike me, he kept his word and was there when he said he'd be. Even when I failed to keep appointments, Stan kept trying. From the first meeting to now, that hasn't changed. But I have.

The last seven or so years can be described as chaos. I have experienced brief stays at more than suitable supported accommodation, intertwined with extended bouts of homelessness, offending and five months in prison. I was given chance after chance but never grabbed it, due to drink, drugs and poor decision making. Even with Stan's support and advocacy, inevitably my actions and behaviour resulted in eviction.

Despite my failures, Stan kept coming back. I always enjoyed catching up with him but often wondered why he didn't give up on me. Before, during and after prison, he was always there…

My downward spiral continued. I got into more and more trouble. My reliability got worse, but Stan was still making time to meet me. The court appearances became more frequent. It was all silly stuff, linked to my drink-and-drug-fuelled lifestyle.

Inevitably things got more serious, and in May 2019 I assaulted someone. I spent the next five months in prison. Stan kept in touch and still had faith in me. Even when I was released from prison, I still didn't get it. I spiralled further into criminal behaviour.

Despite my circumstances, I was still able to link up with Stan. I accessed supported accommodation during lockdown. Sadly, my inability to manage led to more bad choices. I attracted the wrong influences. Drugs took hold, and I became addicted to Crack Cocaine.

I continued in my chaotic ways, 'burning bridges' and oblivious to where I was heading. I experienced extended periods of home-lessness, interspersed with brief support from supported accommodation providers.

Stan was still in contact. The cycle continued. I was evicted again and homeless for a period, before I was given more chances in supported accommodation, followed by more bad decisions and drug use.

I soon ended up on the street and sofa-surfing and had another brush with the police and courts. Stan still made time to meet me. Someone sowed a seed by telling me about recovery and abstinent housing. I thought it would look good in court so I gave it a go.

There I found myself amongst people wanting to quit drugs and, to a certain extent, I saw the light. I discovered a peer group that enabled me to like who I was – and despite my learning disability, I could grasp the idea of friendship. It wasn't easy and Stan was always there, giving me encouragement and keeping me focused.

That takes me up to late 2022. To cut a long story short, we're now in 2024 and I'm drug free. My relationship with my sister, my dad and his partner has gone from dire to great, and I have a really good circle of friends.

Yes, support services have been intervening now and then, but the one constant has been Stan. He's still there, and his support has been immense, but now it's different. I don't see him for support, I see him because I enjoy our catch-ups.

I really don't know where I'd have ended up without him.

I still enjoy being a volunteer mentor but things can be very challenging these days, due to government cutbacks on the prison service and support for charities. Some volunteers get overloaded and decide to give up, and charities struggle when they are expected to take the place of government workers. Volunteers are there to provide additional support, not to replace paid government staff.

The ACE Team, from the left: Amy (caseworker), Anne (volunteer), Sharon (retired manager), me (volunteer), Gary (current manager), John (caseworker) and Charles (caseworker).

CHAPTER 8

On the Road

Life as a travelling salesman, 1990s to 2012

As a freelance self-employed person, I worked as an agent for a company that made loose furniture covers for sofas and so on. My role was to find customers and measure up their furniture, then deliver and fit the covers. I advertised in local papers and got business all over Cumbria. This turned out to be a very lucrative business and I even extended my horizons to the Western Isles of Scotland – the isle of Skye and the Outer Hebrides, Isla and Jura. This gave me the opportunity to explore the Western Isles. I always got a very warm welcome from my customers and made this trip around four times a year, staying about a week in various B and Bs.

I loved the mountainous scenery and the very slow, quiet way of life. The islanders were so friendly – I always got a cup of tea and often a meal while I was measuring their furniture. I was often there for a couple of hours so I got to know them quite well. I was impressed by the very white beaches on the Isle of Harris, Berneray and Benbecula. I would make time to do some walking in between my appointments – and I would go into the local pub for a whisky, especially on Isla and Jura. On Isla I went to the distillery. They gave me a tour and I sampled a wee dram or two! I still like the odd whisky.

Donald Caskie originally came from the village of Bowmore and he's buried there so I went to his grave to pay my respects. His niece was living on the island so I also went to visit her. We talked about Donald for a long time – she asked me what he was like when I'd known him in Paris. She was very friendly and we have stayed in touch ever since.

I continued with this work until 2012. At the same time, I was running a bed and breakfast at my house in Penrith. I was busy but I like being busy. It keeps me going.

CHAPTER 9

Almost Missing My Eightieth Birthday
Paris, 2018

I arranged to have my eightieth birthday in Paris with my niece Trish and her then partner Rob and her son Jason, a friend from South Korea, called Seryoung, and another friend, Hugh, who I'd met at the Scots Kirk, Paris. Hugh often played the piano at Sunday morning worship and he was working as an accountant for Johnson & Johnson in Paris at the time and spoke fluent French.

A buffet was laid on at the Kirk for my eightieth, on the Sunday after morning worship. I arrived in Paris two days before that, and I was able to show Trish, Rob and Jason around the city but I wasn't feeling very well. By Saturday, I was feeling worse. I got up and had breakfast and Seryoung arrived, all the way from Korea, and then Hugh arrived a bit later from Reading.

After breakfast, I was feeling very tired so I went back to bed and said I would see them later at the Irish Pub, close to the hotel, in Montmartre. In the afternoon, I went to meet them at the pub and we talked about booking a birthday meal. After that I had another rest at the hotel and returned to the pub in the early evening and had to tell them that I didn't feel up to going out for dinner. Hugh suggested that they walk me back to the hotel and I was struggling to catch my breath. Hugh got so worried that he wanted to phone an ambulance and I reluctantly agreed.

The ambulance duly arrived at the hotel and after filling in some paperwork they put me on a stretcher and took me to l'Hopital Lairboisière, just behind the Gare du Nord. Only one person was allowed to travel with me so I chose my friend Hugh, as he spoke French so well.

Then there was a bit of a drama. The ambulance driver stopped on the way and requested 300 Euros and explained to Hugh that this was normal procedure. He said I would be able to claim the fee back and apologised for not giving me a receipt. Apparently the ambulance is only free if requested by a doctor, or so he said. Obviously I didn't know this and I didn't have that amount of cash on me. So we were driven to the nearest cashpoint, where I drew 300 Euros from the hole in the wall. It seemed like a scene from a black comedy! It was lucky I wasn't having a serious heart attack and I never did get that money back. I suspect it went into the ambulance driver's pocket.

When we reached the hospital, the staff were brilliant and got me straight into Emergency, or *Urgence* as it's called in France. They made me comfortable on a trolley in the reception area. This must have been about 11:30pm and the hospital consultant realised I was about to turn 80. I remember at midnight the consultant came to my bedside with four or five staff, carrying lighted candles and they sang me Happy Birthday or *Joyeux Anniversaire*!

After routine checks, I was diagnosed with acute pneumonia and admitted to a ward. The staff were excellent – very supportive and most of them spoke English.

I happened to be wearing a large watch (which I still have, and it always attracts attention). On this occasion, a young French medical student said, in broken English, 'If you die before ze morning, please can I 'ave your watch?' When he came to see me in the morning, he found me still very much alive! He explained that he was leaving for Japan and I told him he wouldn't be getting my watch after all. He wished me well.

I didn't have travel insurance because it would have been too expensive, due to my asthmatic problems. Trish, Rob and Jason were booked to leave on the Eurostar after the Sunday celebrations but Jason (aged 33) stayed over because he didn't want to leave me alone in Paris.

On the Sunday, my birthday celebration was cancelled as I was still in hospital and Trish and Rob went home. However, I knew Jason needed to get back to his job as a plumber so the next day I told the consultant I wanted to discharge myself. She pleaded with me to stay. She asked if I was worried about the hospital bill. I said it was a concern – and she explained that, after the first week, it would only cost me 22 Euros per day if I stayed on.

Nevertheless, I refused to change my mind and told her I was definitely leaving. She asked someone to come and dismantle all the drips I was on, mainly oxygen. She said I was taking a big risk and she would arrange for paramedics to meet me at St Pancras and I would probably need to be admitted to hospital as soon as I arrived.

Jason was upset that I was taking such a risk for his sake but I was determined to go. They put me in a wheelchair to take me to the Gare du Nord, no doubt thinking I was mad. However, I travelled with Jason and the journey wasn't too bad. At St Pancras, the paramedics were there to check me over and they gave me the option of going to a hospital in London. Alternatively, they could give me oxygen to last the journey to Penrith by train. I chose the latter.

At Penrith, I had Assistance booked and my other niece, Ruth, came to meet us. We went to A&E in Penrith and they checked me over and said I was very poorly and would need to be admitted to the Cumberland Infirmary in Carlisle. I was in hospital in Carlisle for three or four weeks.

Meanwhile, I learned that I'd had lots of visitors from the Scots Kirk in Paris, including the new minister, Reverend Steyne from South Africa. They had all arrived at L'Hopital Lairboisière. They had visited after I had discharged myself and they must have wondered what was going on. They'd heard I had acute pneumonia but I was nowhere to be found!

CHAPTER 10

All Aboard!

Getting out and about, 2018 onwards

Once I turned eighty, I decided to stop driving and start using public transport. This was a major change to my lifestyle after driving all those miles every year. However, I soon got used to more relaxing and less stressful ways of travelling and I was able to continue with my voluntary work, meeting new people and making new friends on my journeys. I didn't have the worry of parking problems anymore. I travel regularly from Penrith

Ellie and Stan in Glasgow.

Station these days, mainly to Preston and Lancaster where I carry out my voluntary work. I always get a warm, friendly greeting from all the staff at Penrith Station, and I've made new friends there, particularly Ellie, Jenny and Steve. In 2023 I had a day in Glasgow with Ellie, where we enjoyed an Irish coffee in the Irish Bar.

I'm always grateful for the help I get on my travels from people of all ages and walks of life. If they see me struggling, they always offer help, which I appreciate. If I stop for a breather, people will ask me if I'm all right. I have a walking frame, for support, and a stick if I need it – and a wheelchair when necessary. But I try to walk if I can because it's good to keep active and get some exercise.

I attend Remembrance Sunday every year at the London Cenotaph. Unfortunately, these days, I struggle to do the march down Whitehall, Birdcage Walk, and back to Horse Guards Parade, where we are met by a Senior Royal, so

SSAFA provide a volunteer to wheel me round. It's quite emotional, being part of a group of 10,000 or more, paying our respects to the war dead. I enjoy meeting old comrades and making new friends, and London taxis give us free transport to and fro. I always feel very privileged and proud to be part of the organisation.

In 2022, I went to the Remembrance Sunday ceremony with Diana, a colleague from SSAFA.

SSAFA and the British Legion pay for our stay at the Union Jack Club in London.

I have been a volunteer caseworker with SSAFA since 2004. In 2014, I received an official 'Thank You Letter' and a pin badge for completing 10 years' service. Being a hands-on volunteer brings you face to face with some very sad situations. For instance, you may see people living in awful poverty. When you go into someone's home, you have to keep an eye out for signs, such as threadbare carpets, or someone struggling to move around their home because they need a stair-lift or a walk-in wet room. We must never forget that these veterans served our country. I not currently working as a caseworker but I am still involved as a member and look forward to joining the parade at the Cenotaph in London on Remembrance Sunday every year.

In April 2024, I visited Paris as an eighty-sixth birthday present to myself. I normally spend my birthday in Paris but this time I was accompanied by my niece Trish who supported me with my mobility issues and wheeled me round Paris in a wheelchair. Although I was able to do some walking with the aid of a walker, we used buses to visit various places.

We went to the British Hospital where I did my National Service and I made myself known to the staff, as all my previous contacts had moved on or passed away. When I explained the purpose of my visit, I was made very welcome. They were interested to hear about the history of the hospital. I asked if I could visit the private garden dedicated to Sir Richard Wallace, the British philanthropist who founded the hospital for the poor people of Paris, back in the late 1800s. He also provided the spectacular drinking water fountains that are still used all over the city. For me this was quite an emotional visit that brought back memories of my time as a youth in the late 1950s.

My niece Trish and I, standing in front of a Wallace drinking fountain in a private garden at the British Hospital, in a space dedicated to the late Sir Richard Wallace, founder of the hospital.

I also visited the hostel for homeless men in Rue Violet where I once volunteered. I wanted to say hello to Brother Michel who used to manage the hostel. However, I discovered that he now runs a hostel for the homeless in Romania. Nevertheless, we had a long doorstep conversation with a colleague who was very apologetic about not being able to invite us in, because the premises were being sprayed to deal with a bed bug infestation!

Another highlight was Sunday morning worship at the Scots Kirk, in the Rue Bayard. It was good to meet old friends from the congregation. Unfortunately many members have passed away but it was encouraging to see that they had been replaced by new, younger faces. I soon got chatting and made new friends who were very interested to learn a bit of history.

Members of the Scots Kirk congregation, with Trish in the front row and me in the middle, at the back.

Trish and I enjoying our lunch at Les Deux Magots.

They were holding their Annual General Meeting immediately after morning worship so I was able to get the latest update on church business. After the AGM, which didn't last too long, tea, coffee and biscuits were served so we enjoyed meeting and mingling with the congregation. Currently, the church does not have a minister. However, the Very Reverend Colin Sinclair, a locum from Edinburgh, led morning worship and Holy Communion. We sang 'Be still for the presence of the Lord', one of my favourite hymns.

After church on Sunday, our last day in my beautiful Paris, we took the bus towards Notre- Dame and alighted at Boulevard Saint-Michel and had a late lunch at Les Deux Magots. I had a delicious ham and cheese Croque Monsieur. This was one of my favourite haunts in the late fifties and our visit brought back happy memories of that long-gone smoke-filled bar once frequented by 'ladies of the night', homosexuals, artists and eccentrics

I have a big family and we enjoy getting together.

I've always been very close to my great-nephew Jason, who is the son of my niece Trish. He now runs his own business as a plumber and lives in Manchester. When he was younger, he took time off and went to Australia and found some work with a furniture removal company. There he met his fiancée Chiara who is from Venice.

They got engaged while visiting Hawaii – and in January 2024 he became a very proud dad to baby Alma. In February 2024, Chiara's family came over to visit me in Penrith.

We are all looking forward to a very special wedding and christening in Venice in August 2024.

With the family at the George Hotel, Penrith, in February 2024. From the left, my niece Gillian, me, Alberto (Chiara's dad), Trish, Jason and Chiara, with baby Alma.

Me with Elveretta, Chiara's mum.